An Ordinary Girl with an Extra Ordinary Gift

Stephanie Carr

Copyright © Stephanie Carr 2016

Published by East Anglian Press

Disclaimer
This is a true story and entirely from the author's
perspective. Whilst the information in this book are
believed to be true and accurate at the date of going
to press, neither the author nor the publisher can
accept any legal responsibility or liability for any
errors or omissions that may have been made.

British Library Cataloguing in Publication Data.

A CIP catalogue record for this book is available from
the British Library.
ISBN: 978-0-9954844-4-3

Acknowledgements

Many thanks to:

Carol Windsor for permission to use photograph of Horley Spiritualist Church

Cover Creator: Suzan Collins

Proof Reader: Katie Philips

Illustrator: Lynne Rooney

Dedication

I would like to dedicate this book to my family and to everyone that continues to support myself and my work.

My sincere thanks to my husband Tim for whom without his help and support this book would not have happened.

Contents

"Mummy, mummy, come quick, you said Uncle Charlie had died, but he's not, he is in his garden, come and see."

This was my earliest memory that something was a little different with me.

Childhood

I was born at 2pm on July 20th on a hot Friday summer's day in 1962, making me the last child to my mother Vivienne and father Ron.

My oldest sister Heather was their first child and is eleven and a half years older than me, then came Terry my brother, followed by another two sisters Christine and Hazel. I was born in Ipswich, Suffolk, mum gave birth to me at home, which was a three bedroom mid terrace council house and this remained my home till the age of eighteen.

My father had a bit of a drink problem and although his behaviour at times impacted on the whole family, mum managed to keep everything together. When dad wasn't on a binge, he would love working in his garden and took great pride in nature and his flowers. He won many garden competitions of Ipswich in Bloom which meant the world to him.

I was a chubby child, confident, but also quiet. I had a few friends locally that I played with and three sisters that were ordered to take me with them when they went out, so I was never lonely.

It all started at around the age of four. I can remember I was sitting in my beautiful back garden by the fish pond. I looked up over the fence to see if my friends were in their garden playing. I saw their father looking down at the pet tortoise they had, it was called chippy and it was kept at the bottom of their garden on a piece of string that was pulled through a hole on its shell. It would often escape into our garden and I would pick it up and shout, "Uncle Charlie, I have your tortoise." But on this day things were very different, the tortoise hadn't escaped, but there, as clear as day stood, Uncle Charlie! This really surprised me because my mum and dad had told me a few

8

weeks previously that he had died and gone to heaven. He seemed very clear to me at the time and I called out to him, "Uncle Charlie!" (He wasn't really my true uncle, but in those days all my parents friends where known as uncle and auntie.)

Uncle Charlie didn't look when I initially called his name but shortly afterwards he did look at me for what seemed a very brief glance, but it was more like he looked through me. I immediately ran in to tell my parents what had just happened.

"But mum," I said, "I just saw Uncle Charlie!"

"Stephanie, you did not see Uncle Charlie and I will only tell you once, do not talk about death."

My parents were very strict, as parents were in the 60s and 70s and told me not to talk about death.

I remember this time because of the frustration I felt of not being believed was immense to me. The thought of my parents thinking I was lying or making it up hurt me very much. I ran and got the camera out of the drawer of the sideboard we had in our front room, which was a daring thing in itself as we were not even allowed in the front room until after dinner in the evening. It was far too neat and tidy for children to play around in. I ran outside with my heart thumping so hard I thought dad was going to tell me off as I handed him the camera,

"Please Dad, take the picture, you'll see him."

Dad didn't take a picture. No one did. In my little young head I hoped it would come out on a picture. I was desperate for them to believe me, but Mum was so cross with what I was saying and doing. I remember not being allowed back into the garden until I promised there would be no more episodes like this. I felt so sad for not being believed. Looking back I think they were too busy with five children, or just did not have the understanding of what was going on with me, to consider what I was saying might just be true and how their comments made me feel.

***

I started school at the age of five. I was up at around 5am being far too excited to sleep, I got myself washed and dressed and sat on the side of my bed which seemed like a lifetime till everyone started to wake at 7am.

"Crickey Steph! You're keen." My dad said as he passed my room on the way to the bathroom.

I must admit by the time I had my breakfast, I was starting to feel tired and was ready for a little snooze with my dummy that mum and dad were still not able to prise away from me.

"No time for that now," mum said, "Go get your satchel." My dad stood at the front door, I can remember it to this day, tea towel over his shoulder while he waved good luck to me, while my oldest sister Heather and my mum walked me literally across the road to my new infant's school. I remember holding their hands so tight and remember thinking, I really don't want to go to school after all and I began to cry.

"Come and say hello to your new teacher." my mum said, in such a gentle way.

"Hello Stephanie, I am your teacher, and I am going to be looking after you." I never answered, I just cried as she loosened the grip I had on my mother and my sister's hand.

Over the weeks I began to settle in and enjoy school. I made friends easily, but I didn't mind playing on my own either.

I loved assembly, the singing and praying even at the age of 5 resided somewhere deep in me and I would sing my heart out so loud hoping that my mum and dad, if they were in their garden, would hear me. I would run home at lunchtime and ask, "Did you hear me singing today?"

"Yes Stephanie," mum would reply. "You sounded beautiful."

Looking back now I realise that she couldn't have heard me.

The first ever book I crazed my parents for was a picture book about Jesus. I have to say that I still have that very same book and to this day have no idea why I loved biblical stories so much, but I was fascinated about Jesus and his healing powers and the wonders he performed even at such a young age. With this all in mind, mum agreed to let me join Sunday school. This was a little Baptist church right next door to my school, again just across the road.

I liked Sunday school because for me it was a way of getting out the house and being around other children. My Sunday school teacher would always bring a packet of aniseed ball sweets and after our teachings would allow us one each. I loved being in the church, it was cool with the cold stone walls and the candles and the surroundings made me feel very still and calm, in my head and mind at the age of 5, this was a very special place indeed to me.

Aged 5

I really can't remember anything else happening or seeing another spirit as a child again. My father as I have mentioned previously was a drinker and life as a child was difficult and money was very tight. Dad was always in and out of trouble and if there was anything different about me, I feel sure it would have gone unseen with all the other things we as a family had going on.

My sisters spoilt me and to this day still do to a point. In the times I didn't want to join them out with their friends I would often busy myself in trying to make scent out of the dead head petals that fell from the flowers in our garden. This would be around the age of 7 or 8. I would also spend hours trying to catch butterflies to put in a jar, but would then cry as I felt I had to let them go and couldn't watch them trapped. My parents had a little toy poodle and his name was Fluffy, because he was so small and white and yes you guessed it very fluffy. I loved this little dog and many hours would be spent grooming and cuddling him and sometimes I was allowed to walk him around the block on my own.

As I have mentioned I was a chubby child and would often get bullied in school because of my weight. My nick name was Bunty after the chubby girl in the comic. I feared sports day. I participated in games as we had no choice and was always last in everything from the egg and spoon race to the three legged race. I struggled in many subjects and it was often written in my school reports that I was a happy child who cares about many things, but her spelling will always let her down. (It wasn't until I was in my forties that I was diagnosed with dyslexia.) I enjoyed the Religious Education (RE) classes and loved the stories of Jesus. I did very well in typing, cooking and needlework, but had no idea on what I wanted to do when leaving school. My maths wasn't too bad.

One day in primary school we were all waiting for the bell to ring to indicate to us it was home time, my teacher started asking some of the children, "What would you like to be when you grow up?"
All different answers came from the class.

"I'm going in the army Sir," was one reply,

"I'm going to be a hairdresser Sir," was another.

"And you Stephanie, what about you? What do you want to do when you grow up?"

"I'm going to be a nun, Sir."

The class gasped, there was a moments silence, which seemed an eternity, then a roar of laughter from everyone, including a grin from Sir and I could not understand why they were laughing or what they found so funny. I remember thinking 'what is so funny, why don't you want to be more linked to Jesus and to be kind and gentle in this world?'

I was saved or so I thought with the sound of the bell and without even a dismissal, everyone got up and started to hurry out of what was a porta cabin that contained our class room.

"Stephanie wants to be a nun." The children started to shout and tease as we walked down the path that would lead us to the exit gate of our school. I would feel my face going bright red and my heart would pound as people laughed and took the 'Micky' for days. I realised then, at that moment, at the age of 7 that maybe mum telling me to 'Shhh' and not to speak about things like that was what I had to do to prevent this teasing, so for most of my school life that is exactly what I did.

Aged 8

At the age of around 10 I was allowed to walk to the next few roads on the estate alone and play with a few friends who were in my school.

I became aware on how my friends were feeling and seemed to know exactly what was bothering them, without them uttering a word.

When calling for my friend for school one morning she seemed quieter and I said.

"Your dad will say sorry tonight for flying at you over dinner last night."

"How do you know?" my friend asked.

I shrugged my shoulders. "I don't know." And I didn't. I had no idea how I knew, or why I had even said it. A few moments later we would be joking and laughing. "You're spooky, you are." was her reply and as if the conversation had never taken place we were on our way to school talking about something else.

Later that night whilst we were out playing my friend said, "You were right Steph, my dad said 'sorry'."

I tried telling my mum about this and she said. "Stephanie, what you see and feel is part of growing up, but you must be careful how you speak, you don't want them doctors in big white coats coming to lock you away for hearing voices."

This was yet another constraint in my young mind, to keep quiet and keep things in! I also began to have strange dreams and in these dreams there was another me talking back at me.

Allow me to explain. Ever since my teens I have changed my hair colour from my natural colour, light brown to blonde or dark red, this change happens every couple of months and has remained right up till now. However sometimes when I look in the mirror, I see a vision of myself looking back at me and it is with my natural mousy brown colour. One day while sitting on my own with my mum I mentioned this. She smiled and said very casually, "Maybe it is your twin."

18

"Twin?" I asked in complete shock, "What twin?"

"You were an identical twin, but the other baby did not live and was wrapped up quickly and taken away at birth."

This was the first time I had knowledge of this, I felt my jaw drop, and was in total surprise and shock at what my mother had just told me.

"Why haven't you told me this before?"

"Well I am telling you now," she said, "Anyway it was a long time ago, and you didn't really need to know, did you?"

I sat mouth still wide open at her flippant response. I had no idea of any of this. I was aware my Granddad was a twin, but he had died the month before I was born in June 1962 and I was told by my mother that it was him who chose the name Stephanie.

I was very shocked at finding this news out, but maybe this was the reason for my dreams and visions of seeing myself.

When my periods started at thirteen my senses became heightened. I would feel my friend's pain and upset as if it was my own. I would feel so sad for my father and his dependence on drink, even though my thoughts and loyalties should have been more for my mother who was busting a gut to look after us all and keep us safe while my father struggled with his addiction. I somehow saw her as the strong one and my father as the weaker one.

I also started to have dreams that would come real the next day. I remember standing in the sweet shop on the way to school and in walked a neighbour and said. "Hello Stephanie how is your mum? I haven't seen her in a while."

She then reached over the counter for a sherbet dip. "There you go darling, a little treat from me."

I looked at her and remembered straight away that I had dreamt this conversation the night before in every little detail. This really scared me and I began to feel dizzy. The next thing I knew I was being taken home in a car by the owner after passing out in my local paper shop. I tried to tell mum what had happened, but her reply was. "Stephanie, you are starting your periods, a lot of girls will go dizzy and pass out, it's your body changing and please don't keep going on about these dreams."

As the period came to the end of its monthly cycle all would be calm again.

As time went on in my teens I did start to see spirit. At first I would look and think, is it a shadow or a reflection and look around to see who was there to be projecting it. The more solid it became the less of a person I would see. It was like a shadow of a full person, or just a side of face or top half. Very different to how I see living people. I honestly thought at the time that everyone could see this.

When my friends asked, "What are you looking at Steph?"

I would answer, "The shadow, can't you see it?"

"Oh shut up," would be the reply, "I can't see anything, stop trying to scare us!"

So I soon learnt that they couldn't see what I saw. I told myself not to mention anything or they would tease me again.

Although I didn't speak much any more about what I saw and felt, those friends that where closest to me soon caught on to certain things I would do and say with a slip of the tongue and I was soon labelled with the nick name 'Spooky Steph', this however was said more in jest then cruelty.

When I wasn't at school I would play with my friends doing normal childhood girly stuff, like hanging around street corners, giggling and talking about boys, makeup and hair, all the things that young girls do, although I had to be in at 8pm every night. I would never ever dare be late, not even by a minute. I was never allowed to stay at a friend's house for sleep-overs.

My oldest sister Heather lived in the next road to us and I would often go to her home on Sunday afternoon after Sunday school. She would allow me to cook things for her like sausage rolls and jam tarts. I loved baking but wasn't really allowed to do it in mum's kitchen as this was her spot along with mum's, "Don't make a mess Stephanie" and the waste of ingredients if it all went terribly wrong, which it sometimes did. It just made it easier for her to do all the cooking and me to do my experimenting at my sister's home. Heather was happy to allow me to do this, because most of the time, my cooking actually turned out quite nice.

Because my family life as a child was quite difficult with my father being a drinker, little things about my gift and feelings were gone unnoticed. With mum doing the very best she could with five children to look after, trying to make ends meet and feeding us with very little money coming in to the house was a constant struggle for her, even our school work was overlooked.

At the age of thirteen and while I was at Westbourne High School I met Tim. The first time I clapped eyes on him my heart missed a beat. He was taller than all the other boys in our year, with a thick head of blonde hair and blue eyes. He was a popular boy, with a distinctive loud laugh. I made it known to some of my friends that I liked him and soon the word got around. The most that happened would be a smile as we passed in the corridor for a while, but within a week or two this changed. This particular day I was on my way to my classroom. I passed Tim and done the normal shy smile and started to walk up the cold stone stairs to get to my form class. Tim had done a back turn and followed me. "Steph" he called, again my heart skipped a beat and I turned to see this tall, young and very good looking boy standing in front of me. I could feel my face going so red I thought it was going to burst and this was the very first time we had ever spoke, "Yes." I answered.

"What you doing Saturday?" he asked. By now I could feel myself shaking from the inside, right down to my, by now, hot sweaty hands.

"Nothing."

"You are now." said this confident young boy, the rest is history, we started dating at the age of 13 and have stayed together ever since.

Aged 15

Leaving home

I left school in 1978 at the age of 16, without a qualification to my name. My mother read out a job that was advertised in the local paper 'The Evening Star.'

"Stephanie," my mum said, "Tooks Bakery are advertising for an admin assistant, I think you should go for it." Tooks was in walking distance to where I lived and I started to get a little excited, "What does admin entail?" I asked.

"Well I reckon it is typing and office duties. You always got good reports at school for typing," she replied, "but you won't know unless you go and find out." Mum wrote the number down on a torn piece of old paper and sent me round to Ulster Avenue which was where the nearest telephone box was.

With my hands shaking I dialled the number and a polite lady answered.

"I am phoning about the job as admin assistant," I said with a trembling voice.

"Hold on I'll put you through to the admin manager" she replied. Within minutes a man was on the end of the phone and I found myself repeating what I had just said.

"Do you have any experience?" he asked.

"No," I replied, "I have just left school."

"Okay, come up and see me at 2 o'clock Friday afternoon for an interview."

The excitement in my voice as I said thank you was so high pitched you would have thought he had offered me the job there and then. I ran home so fast, I nearly fell in through the back door. "I got an interview mum, on Friday, I'm so excited."

Mum was sitting in the kitchen still drinking a half cup of tea which she had been drinking when I left.

"It's really good you have an interview," she replied, "But try not to get too excited, there will be lots of people going for the job and an interview doesn't mean you will get it. It felt like she had just popped my bubble right there, in an instant. "I know," I replied, pretending I understood that already, but inside I was still positive that this job was mine.

So on the Friday I dressed in my best clothes and listened to all the advice my mum told me on how I should conduct myself and the answers I should give when certain questions were asked.

I arrived at Tooks Bakery and as I walked up to the entrance the smell of fresh bread and cakes was overwhelming. I could live working with this smell I thought to myself, as a cheeky smile came over my face. I waited at the reception after saying who I was and felt my hands becoming very sweaty. Within a very short time I was led through the main office where around twenty other women of all ages sat, and I could feel every eye on me as I walked through, being led to a smaller room in the corner of the office. Once again I felt my face going red hot and I hadn't even met the manager yet.

He was very charming and friendly and I was soon put at ease.

"So Stephanie, you have just left school?"

"Yes," I replied.

"What subjects did you take and what CSE results do you think you will get?"

My heart sank. "I don't think I am going to do very well," Mum would have a fit if she could hear me now. "But I love typing." I quickly said, trying to follow up with a positive answer. "And I only live round the corner so I would be able to walk to work." As if that was really going to seal the deal.

"So tell me Stephanie, why you think I should give this job to you?"

"Because I really, really want it," I said, "And I promise I will work so hard for you." He smiled as if he didn't expect that answer, but the truth was, that was all I could offer.

"Okay. I still have a few people to see, but I will let you know."

The next few days came and went and on the Tuesday I still hadn't heard anything and mum said, "I still have the phone number, go and call them, at least you will know one way or the other."

So yet again I was sent to the phone box to make the call.

This time I was not so nervous and I made the call asking to speak to the Administration Manager.

"Hello," I said, "It's Stephanie, I came for an interview Friday."

"Oh yes," he replied, "Sorry Stephanie I've been so busy I haven't even got around to sorting anything out yet."

"Oh Okay," I replied and he must have heard the disappointment in my voice, as I was thinking of the continuing next few days of waiting to still hear if I got the job.

"Tell you what," he said, "Because you are so keen, the job is yours"

"REALLY?" I shouted.

"Don't let me down. We will see you at 9 O'clock Monday morning."

Well, by the time I got home I was the most excited I had ever been in my whole life.

"I GOT IT!" I screamed to my mum, who calmly looked at me and said.

"I thought you might."

I stayed working at Tooks for the next ten years until I fell pregnant with my first child Aaron at the age of twenty five.

At the age of eighteen, after working at Tooks for two years due to dad's drinking, I found myself in yet another big argument with him, with poor mum stuck in the middle.

"Get out," he shouted, so I did and I went to my sisters.

"I really don't want to go back!" I sobbed.

"Well don't," she replied. "You can stay here for a while, until you find yourself somewhere else to live."

Within a day or so, dad had calmed down and was asking me to go home. But I knew if I did, within a week, the same pattern of rows would continue and that just wasn't fair on anyone.

After a few weeks had passed along with some sleepless nights on my sister's sofa she showed me a cutting in the newspaper, of a bedsit to rent. Tim came with me to look at it as I didn't want to go by myself.

We turned up at the very creepy looking house. It had three floors and nine rooms, three large communal bathrooms that everyone had to

30

share. I was led to the bedsit at the very top of the house, which was £13.00 per week and I was earning £22.00 a week.

"I don't like it," I whispered to Tim. "It's dark and creepy and cold." (And the only window was so high up like a sky hatch I don't think I could have reached it if I tried.)

We were offered another room which was four times bigger than we had just seen, instead of a single bed there was a large double and a place to keep all my clothes, a fridge and a large table and chairs. I wanted to cry as this would be perfect for me as I had no furniture, but knew I just couldn't afford it.

"She will take it," Tim said.

"I can't afford it," I whispered.

"I'll help you," he replied and then asked,

"Where does she sign?"

I moved in within a few days and got myself a little wooden rocking chair to sit on. Tim had previously brought me a black and white portable telly for my 18th Birthday and I used to sit on my little chair watching telly in my own home and to me this was my little palace. I also brought a white budgie in a cage to keep me company. Tim and I became engaged very soon after in the October of 1980.

I think this was more reassurance for me that he was going to stick around to support me and wasn't going anywhere.

I spent three happy years there until Tim and I brought our first property, a bungalow in April 1983, aged 20.

I moved in straight away as I was unable to afford the mortgage and rent on my bedsit. A few weeks passed and Tim and I were busy painting our new home and putting our stamp on our place, when he said,

"How do you fancy a June or July wedding?"

I was taken aback. "That's only two months away," I replied. "It doesn't leave us much time."

"Well there is no need to hang about now we have a home and paying a mortgage." he said.

So we did, on July 30th 1983 ten days after my 21st birthday, at St Thomas Church I became Mrs S Carr, one of the happiest days of my life.

Tim came from a very strong family unit. His father Ken was a lovely gentle kind man, very much like Tim and worked most of his life on the British Rail. His mother Dorothy was very much family orientated, with strong Christian beliefs. She would attend church every Sunday and do the flowers for the church weddings and christenings most weekends. She also busied herself making many things for the church annual bazaar.

His family was very much calmer than mine and I soon became aware of just how different life as a family could be without the strains of alcoholism.

Tim also has a younger sister of seven years, being Ken and Dorothy's only two children and although his mother didn't quite get or understand my family's position or strains, I was always made to feel very welcome into their home and family. I very soon started attending Church with my mother-in-law Dorothy, at St Thomas, this was something again I loved. I would always feel so at peace in a church, and I had actually been christened and married in this one. It was by far the biggest I had attended, it had a grand alter leading to the foot of where hung the most beautiful gold brass cross, with candles underneath. This was also nice because I was attending it with Tim's mum and after service every Sunday we would be invited back to her home for the best Sunday lunch ever. Tim would always be off playing football on a Sunday morning and the family would all come together for Sunday roast at around one.

The more I got involved with the church and the Bible readings at this age, the more and more confused I became.

I was horrified, worried and very much saddened to read in the Bible that mediums where seen as evil and people that witness spirit or heard voices should be stoned to death. This implanted in me, even more, that I should not speak at all about what I was seeing and hearing. Yet again, my mum's voice rang clear in my mind, "You must not talk in that way Stephanie or those men in white coats will take you away!"

So I didn't and for many years, all the things I felt and saw I kept very much in and didn't share.

However, there was always a question lurking in the back of my mind. I saw myself as a kind ordinary girl, that would help anyone, I had never dabbled in anything dark, like witch craft, Ouija boards, or with any negative energies and I certainly didn't ask to be born with this insight. Did Jesus himself not also hear voices and speak to spirit? And did he not also want to help in the name of love with people's pain? So what was the difference?

Unfortunately, I didn't understand enough and as I had been told so many times not to go there or mention it, so I didn't.

As I wrote earlier my senses when I was on a monthly cycle would become much stronger. So this also came as a surprise when I fell pregnant in 1986 with my first child Aaron. When I was on a period my emotions and senses were very much heightened, but now not only for a week at a time, this was staying with me for the whole nine month's I carried him!

The things I was seeing and feeling were all becoming impossible to ignore!

I woke one morning and Tim had already got up and gone to work. He was working for Royal Mail and his mornings would start around 4am. *I had a dream and in it our lovely home we were trying to build had water an inch deep in the kitchen coming from our second hand washing machine. I looked for towels to mop it up and as I was trying to soak the water up my front door bell went and as I opened the door there stood the postman with a parcel I had to sign for. I just stared at him! I stretched as I started to wake and become aware of my conscious state.*

I rubbed my eyes and pulled one curtain back from the window to let the light in while I was still able to lie in bed. Still stretching and yawning I dragged myself out of bed on this lovely Saturday sunny morning.

I started to walk to the bathroom and as I did I noticed water in the hall coming from my kitchen, I opened the door and there it was, an inch of water over my kitchen floor from our washing machine. Was this really happening? I had dreamt the very same thing. I stood there frozen.

Get a grip Stephanie. I told myself as I hurried to get towels from the bedroom and as I started to soak the water up my doorbell rang. I stepped over the now soaking towels and reached over to answer my door and there he was the same postman I had seen in my dreams. "Can you sign for this please?" he asked.

I just stood there again frozen,

"I dreamt of you," I said in a soft whisper

He laughed. "Did you? Was it a nice dream?"

Then I remembered another part of the dream. Tim at work and a big cabinet, which looked like a filing cabinet full of letters, was toppling over. I had to phone Tim as soon as I could. I hurriedly signed for the parcel and closed the door. The kitchen floor would have to wait. I went straight to the phone. My hand by now was shaking uncontrollably as I dialled Tim's work number. I remember talking so fast and in a muddle he said. "Whoa! Slow down Steph, start from the beginning." So I did. I told him of the dream and how I had got up and it was all happening and then I said, "I remember seeing in my dream a cabinet in your office toppling over." He was the manager of Felixstowe sorting office at the time. Tim laughed and I heard him shout out to the people in the office.

"Hey guys, you wanna hear this. Steph's on the phone, saying she dreamt the filing cabinet was going over." He put his mouth back closer to the phone and said. 'Steph you should have called around half hour ago, that's when it happened."

Tim laughed, trying to calm me, as he could obviously hear the panic by now in my voice, "You know these things sometimes happen with you, try not to let it worry you too much, it's done now, I won't be too late home and we will see what needs to be done with the floor then."

I came off the phone and just sat there for what seemed an age. Why why, why? I asked myself, for what reason is this happening to me?

My husband has never mocked or made fun of my gift. He says he doesn't know or understand how it works, but over the years has seen too much via me to totally believe and see there is something very much deeper going on with me.

The Loss of My Father

Aaron was born on March 31st 1987, after a long six week stay in hospital for me with Pre- eclampsia he was a healthy 6lb 13oz and again, another one of the happiest days of my life. I had this beautiful little boy with a full head of pure blonde curly hair.

I soon fell pregnant again and within eighteen months in January 1989 my daughter Lucy followed, a sister to Aaron.

In my mind I always only wanted two children and I had got my wish, a son and a daughter. So it came as a massive surprise to us both to find out in 1990 that I was pregnant yet again, with child number three Joshua who was born in the following September, giving us three children under the age of 4.

While I was pregnant with Joshua my father was diagnosed with cancer, aged 59.

He had suffered so much in his last few weeks and I remember looking out of his bedroom window and praying to the heavens, asking, "Is it this hard to die?"

I asked this, not because I wished my father gone, but because over the past few months I had watched his frail body decline, with just a spoonful of food a day, and the odd sip of water. Knowing my father the way I did, he would hate this existence. I was also amazed at how much his body had endured over the last few months.

My belief in the afterlife is absolute and I did not want to see him suffer any more. I also wished peace for my mother and siblings for the pressure his illness had brought to our family.

The night before he passed my father had been in a coma state for four days, but this evening he clearly opened his eyes and looked in a blank space and said, "Mother, father", not mum or dad as he would always address them.

We had all taken turns to sit with him for over a week, night and day around his bed at the family home with just the landing light on to take away the pitch black from his bedroom. The hallway light would flicker uncontrollably at times, yet even after looking at the light switch and changing the bulb, there was no clear reason why this should happen.

My father passed on March 8th 1990 aged 60 and within minutes of his passing the new light bulb went out and never came back on. We all looked at each other taking this as a sign.

After my father passed and his funeral had taken place, I found myself visiting the cemetery every day. It is in the next village to where I live so only took five to ten minutes to get there by car. One particular weekend I couldn't visit as I had been away with Tim and the children but did so on the Sunday when we returned home. "I just need to go and check on dad."

I arrived and opened the big wooden gate that was the entrance to the cemetery, I was all alone and nobody else was in sight. I stood there head down just looking at the flowers that was already laid upon the grass. I remember thinking, "Come on dad, you know what I can see, feel and hear. If you can do anything at all just one thing to show me you're OK and there is something after this life please, please show me."

I returned home and got on with my routine of washing and bathing the children as normal after our weekend away.

The very next morning I awoke with a start and opened my eyes, the light had just started to peep through the curtains as night turned in to another day and it would have been around 5am. I still had the rocking chair in my bedroom that I had had in my bedsit. As my eyes turned to the window, there sat my father, so very clear. He was expressionless and I noticed his hair looked greyer then I remembered.

"Dad!" I gasped.

This image remained for what seemed quite a while and I was nudging Tim to wake up.
"What?!" he answered abruptly at being brought out of his sleep.

"Look, can you see Dad?"

"No." he replied.

Despite this conversation my dad was still sat on the chair. As I stared at him it wasn't as if he faded, but more like the chair become more prominent through him. The whole experience from start to finish lasted 3 or 4 minutes. I couldn't go back to sleep or lay down again, I was totally numb in thought, then I remembered what I had asked for the previous day and I hurried down the stairs to call my sister to tell her what had happened.

"Dad is okay," I told her. "I asked for a sign last night while I was at his grave and this morning when I woke up I saw him sis, as clear as day."

"Really?" she replied, (my sister was fully aware of the things I saw and felt, but we also never really spoke too much about the subject.)

"Yes, the only difference Sis, is his hair looked a little greyer then I remember." Dad was very lucky to always have a full lock of dark black hair that never receded or thinned out as he got older.

She then reminded me that in the last few weeks while he was very unwell his hair did go grey, but because we were all with him looking after him 24/7 it went unnoticed to me at the time.

"Well Sis," I said, "It happened and I now feel very at peace that he was telling me he was OK."

A few days after this I was having a coffee with my friend Kym who I met through work some years back and we have remained friends ever since.

"How are things?" she asked, as she looked at my tummy, I was starting to show with my third child Joshua and she knew I had not long lost my father.

"They are good." I replied with a smile and I felt the need to explain straight away why I was so calm with my answer. "I've seen dad." I blurted out.

She looked at me as if she had lost the trail of conversation, "WHAT?!" she replied.

I found myself explaining to her everything that had happened and I know I had been told all my life not to talk in this way in fear of what people might say or think, but with this, well I really felt I wanted to share it.

"You think I'm nuts don't you?" I asked as I sat back in my chair clasping my coffee cup tight, feeling a little deflated by her non-expression and glare.

"No of course I don't," she replied and took my hand. "Listen." she said, "There is a Spiritualist Church in Ipswich on London Road that do services on a Saturday and Sunday night, I will come with you if you want to go."

"Mn maybe," I said, but little did she know that if my father did have anything he wanted to say, then he could just show or tell me himself. Surely I didn't have to go to some spooky church, after all I was a Christian, even been baptised, this would surely be seen by the Christian Church as very wrong.

I quickly changed the conversation to being pregnant and how big my tummy was getting and the clothes I could no longer fit in. I feel as if I've been pregnant for nearly four years I joked, having had two other children in this time.

As the days and weeks went on I kept thinking about what my friend had said. A church where people also hear see and feel things. My curiosity was getting the better of me. Were there also other people out there who are able to experience the same as me and even more importantly, was it ok to talk about it?

"Have you ever heard of a Spiritual Church?" I asked my mother-in-law a few days later. She had just called round as she often did to take Aaron and Lucy to the park, so I was able to put my feet up for an hour and rest my very swollen pregnant ankles.

I asked this question, more for her reaction then an actual answer. With her being a very Christian lady, if she warns me never to go near one I would try and put all thoughts of going out of my mind.

"Not really," she replied, "I don't think it's a real church, it certainly isn't recognised in the Christian faith. Why?"

"Oh, no reason," I replied and cut the conversation short.

The nagging curiosity didn't leave me and I really did feel I wanted to go and see what this church was all about. Not because I needed or wanted a message from dad or anyone else for that matter... but other people, who saw and felt things like me, well the curiosity was just getting the better of me.

So after a few weeks had passed I phoned Kym.

"Do you still fancy going to this church?" I asked. "It doesn't matter if you don't." I hurriedly added. If she declined my offer, that would be the end of it, because I definitely wasn't going to be going alone.

"Yes of course," she replied. "Let's do it Sunday."

So that was it, the date and time made.

Later that day I mentioned to Tim that I was going out Sunday night with Kym and where we were going but I played it down.

"I'm just going because Kym wants to go and see," I added.

"Okay." he said. "No problem," He didn't ask or seem to have any interest in the church or what it represented.

So the following Sunday came and I went along to the church. Kym picked me up as I had no idea where I was going, or where it was. We arrived in the car park and as I looked at this building I remember laughing saying, "Are you sure this is the right place, it doesn't look anything like a church, it looks more like a village hall!"

As we walked in we were greeted with a smile and handed a hymn book. "First time?" The lady asked.

"Yes," Kym replied.

I just put my head down and tried not to make eye contact as I started to think, "Maybe this was a bad idea and it's wrong for me to be here."

We walked into another room which was the focal point of the church. I picked a seat right at the back where I couldn't be seen and sat down. After a while and becoming a little more relaxed I started to look at my surroundings.

It was just a normal large square room, just like a village hall, but there was definitely an air of peace about this building. On the side of each wall hung four beautiful hand crafted angels, about four feet high, "Faith, Love, Hope and Charity" were the names engraved beneath each angel. "They are beautiful." I said as I nudged Kym's arm.

At the alter was a stage where the service would be conducted and at the foot of it in the middle was, again, the most beautiful crafted wooden pair of praying hands.

On the wall hung a plaque quoting, The Seven Principles of Spiritualism

1. The Fatherhood of God

2. The Brotherhood of Mankind

3. Community of Spirits and Ministry Angels

4. Continued existence of the Soul

5. Personnel Responsibility

6. Compensation and Retribution here after for all the Good and Evil Deeds done on Earth

7. Eternal Progress Open to every Soul.

As I stared reading this wall mounted plaque my eyes kept going back and falling on number 5, 'Personal Responsibility. Is that Personal Responsibility to who we are? I asked myself.

The service started with a song followed by a hymn and The Lord's Prayer. This all feels okay, I told myself. They are praying to the God I know and recognise, so I feel very comfortable with that.

Then a lady, a medium, stood up and for the next hour started to address people who were sitting in the congregation. She would point to a complete stranger and say, "I see your mother or father who is now in spirit, I feel this has been happening around you." And would begin to give full details of happenings of this person's life… "I know you have been sad over the last few days." she continued.

My God. How brave is she, not only is she standing in front of around 80 strangers and sharing with them her thoughts and insights, she has 80 people all ready to hear and listen with no radical or retribution to follow against her. In fact the love and compassion that these messages were bringing was clear to see just how much it was helping the people who received them.

Yet again my eyes would go to the plaque, number 5, "Personal Responsibility to who you are".

I never received a message from my father that night and in fact I really wasn't seeking one. What I did receive from this church was much deeper.

"Maybe, just maybe, my gift wasn't evil, maybe just maybe, instead of being stoned like the Bible had said I should be… standing in my own truth and accepting the gift that I was born with would be me taking personal responsibility for who I am. I could indeed start to acknowledge it and maybe start to use it to help people. After all, I had been born this way and I had never gone out seeking or searching for it. The lady I had just seen had stood in her own truth and was taking personal responsibility for who she was. I had a lot to think about.

By the time I returned home, Tim had already put Aaron and Lucy to bed and all was calm in the Carr household.

"How was it?" he asked.

"Different," I answered. "There was a lady there who took the service, she was like me, she hears things and sees things and she isn't afraid to tell people and to help them. I might go again." I muttered, awaiting for a response or comment from him to whether I should or not.

"Okay," he said, as easy and as calmly as that.

So I did and for many weeks I started to attend the Church every Sunday, listening to a different medium, men and women, address the congregation. They were all very honest and open about what they were hearing and feeling and always with the intent to help and bring peace and guidance to the person they were addressing. The people receiving the message would also show great respect back, there was no ridicule, like my mum or even the Bible had led me to believe!

I went in to hospital in the September to give birth to my son Joshua and for a few weeks I didn't attend church.

I returned to attending the church just before the Christmas of 1990.

"We have missed you," was the welcome I got from the lady who ran the church. "Thank you," I replied and explained how having three children under the age of four was taking up a lot of my time and energy.

"You need to find some time for yourself," she replied. "We have a circle held here on a Tuesday night if you're interested?"

"A circle, what's that?"

"It's a group of around ten to fifteen people. I teach you how to relax, meditate and be open with what you hear, see and feel."

I just stood and looked at her. Did she know I was able to see and hear things myself? Or was she just being nice and was thinking I was looking over tired? I had no real idea and I certainly wasn't about to ask.

"Okay, I will give it some thought,"

That night on returning home I mentioned to Tim what had been said, "What do you think I should do?" I asked him.

"It's up to you, as long as you don't feel too tired after having the children all day, because the evening time is the only rest you really get." he replied.

So the next week I asked to join the circle. Everyone within the circle group was very friendly and all came from different age, sex and backgrounds.

It took me well over a year to learn how to meditate, I used to sit and close my eyes and try to follow and stay with my teacher's voice, but my mind would wander to what to do the children for their packed lunch the next day and would they all be in bed by now. But over time and with lots of practice I mastered it. I was able to channel and see many things in my meditation, such as my twin.

Many people would sit after the sessions and say they saw what they thought to be their guardian. Some would speak of North American Indians, or Chinese doctor's telling them they should follow the path of healing. But for me I never saw anything as grand and to this day still never have. But I do often see myself, my twin, always with normal mousey brown hair, talking, guiding and staring back at me.

I soon became very comfortable with the people within the group and after a meditation session found myself sharing with them all the things I had seen, felt and heard whilst in meditation with sometimes the odd message to follow.

This was okay I convinced myself, I was in a church and I was taking personal responsibility for who I am.

Easter was approaching and at the church on Good Friday an extra service would be held. But instead of a medium coming and conducting the service, it was a chance for all the people who had been sitting in circle, Fledglings we were called, to be invited up on to a platform to use and share our gift to help others.

A few days before Good Friday I visited my mother along with a great big dark chocolate Black Magic Easter egg, her favourite.

"Mum, I have something I need to tell you." I then found myself telling my mother all about the church I was attending and how some other people were just like me.

"They also have the ability and it is not seen as wrong to stand and share these feelings with others."

"But the Bible says it is Stephanie."

I jumped straight back with, "Well then why did God make me this way?"

It was an answer that neither she nor I could answer.

"My darling, you have always spoken in this way and it has never left you. I have only ever wanted to protect you so people didn't think you were mad. But if this church and the people can help and accept you, and you feel safe, then good luck, but please be careful, as I really don't understand enough about it all." Was her very soft reply.

My invitation along with some other's in the group came. "Would you like to Stephanie?" My teacher asked.

"Not sure." I replied.

"Why?" she asked.

"What if I can't, what if they laugh at me?"

I was being asked to do something in public that I had been told all my life not to do.

I remember my teacher's words coming back at me very calmly. "You must take the 'I', as in you Stephanie, out, your gift was given to you to share and help people and if you use it in a good way with a good honest open heart, the rest will follow."

I looked up to the quotation,

Personal Responsibility for who we are.

I answered. "Okay, I will give it a go."

I told Tim when arriving home what I had been asked to do.

"Do you feel okay with doing that?" he asked.

"In all honesty I don't know but there is only one way to find out!" I replied.

So Good Friday came and I can assure you that many times that day I thought of an excuse I could use to get out of the evening.

But the teacher will know it's an excuse, open and honest Stephanie, that's what's been taught.

So I went along. It was going to just be the once I told myself, what harm could it do? The evening started and there were 7 of us all up on the platform. Straight away I was aware and felt not only my own nervousness in the pit of my stomach, but the nervousness of the other six people with me.

My heart was thumping so hard I felt sure everyone would hear it and my hands were cold, wet and clammy. How are you going to be able to help others and have people believe in you, if you don't believe in yourself? I asked myself.

So I closed my eyes and took a few deep breaths just like I had been taught over the years in meditation and there as clear, as clear, was my twin, just smiling back at me.

"Anyone got anything they would like to give?" asked our teacher.

I looked at the other 6 people on the platform, all of which shook their heads and looked down as their nervousness got the better of them. My teacher had worked so hard in trying to install confidence in us all I thought, we owed it to her to at least try.

"I do." I said, as I stood up to take some kind of lead and with a very reassuring smile she offered me the stage and stepped back to resume her place in her chair.

What have I done? I thought to myself. Here I stand in this church I had become accustomed to, with around a hundred people looking at me awaiting for something, anything to come from my mouth.

I scanned the church at all the people that sat before me and as I did, my focus kept going back to a young girl around the same age as me sitting on the 4th row.

Now let me explain how my gift works. I get an overwhelming feeling of a presence. The stronger it is the more I recognise it as male or female. The love that comes with this feeling tells me how close this spiritual energy would be to the person receiving the message. Then the words and sentences come into my mind, far quicker than my own mind or thoughts could register. It is like reading a whole person's life story in seconds, a very strong JUST KNOWING, that I have become accustomed to trust.

"Can I speak to you?" I asked her. I could hear the trembling in my voice.

"Yes." she answered, with a lovely smile that at once put me at ease. I became very aware of her father's energy.

"I have your father here and he also wants to say hello to your mum, his wife."

"This is her." she replied, as she pointed to the older lady that sat beside her and they both started to hold each other's hand in support of one another.

"You're not sleeping well he tells me."

"No," she shook her head.

"And he has just told me he passed with cancer, but he points to his chest and says he doesn't understand why he had an operation after he passed and I know and feel he hasn't been over for very long. He also says he didn't like the machine and mask on his face at the end, and he wants you to remember him, as the strong man he was."

They both gasped in disbelief that I could even know this. The message continued with many facts coming through from her father.

I was told after that the family was upset that their father had had to have a post mortem after he passed. Even though he had been dying of cancer and they didn't expect this to happen, he had previously worked with asbestos and the doctor wanted to see if this had contributed to his cancer.

I was left feeling happy that I had been brave enough to stand up in front of so many people, and to be able for the first time in my life to publicly use my gift to help people.

Family Life

Joshua was only five weeks old when I applied for a job at the local ASDA Store as a checkout operator. This was just a few evenings a week. This helped a little with the funds to run the home, but more so for me as a break from three children under the age of four, to be me again and not just their mum. I was offered the job the day after my interview and was very much looking forward to having adult conversations with people again, since most of my days was filled up with three children not even at school age yet.

So this became my little life. I was a full-time mum during the day working three evenings a week, with one day at the weekend. I still enjoyed sitting in circle on a Tuesday evening whilst attending the church on a Sunday when I could. I even managed to drag Dorothy along, my mother-in-law and my sisters a few times. Dorothy came to see what it was all about but insisted it was more to support me and would be staying with her own Christian church and faith.

In the time I worked at ASDA I climbed the ladder from checkout operator then worked my way through most departments till I reached Training Coordinator. This position entailed me working in the Personnel Department, employing people then training them up on the department they had been chosen to work in. It was a lovely little job and I was still able, at times, to work on platform for the church when asked.

This went on over a ten year period. In the meantime my mother, after losing my father become very unwell. She wasn't a lady that went out and socialised and after dad passed away it became harder for her to leave the house. Because of her own demons and anxieties she became very much a recluse in the remaining 7 years of her life.

I would visit her every day with shopping and the things she would ask me to get her for that day, "20 Number Six" (being her daily packet of cigarettes), a bottle of Lilt and a prawn sandwich became very much the usual items on her list. She struggled greatly with motivating herself to even wash and dress, and even the smallest spark of happiness within her now was hard to see, We, her children almost begged her on a daily basis to see a doctor and try to get some kind of help, but her anxieties had spiralled out of control and were far bigger than us. So our pleas in trying to help her always fell on deaf ears, as she blatantly refused any medical help whatsoever.

I can see now as I have grown older that my mother's life was a hard and sad one. She loved my father with all her heart, she must have done to stay with him all through his drinking and the strain that this had put on her.

I strongly believe that the day my father passed away was the day my mother started to give up. With no fight or drive left in her, the years had taken its toll and she felt she had nothing more to give this world. My mother had osteoporosis of the bones, a family genetic fault my sisters and I have also inherited at a much younger age than usual.

My Mother's Passing, why did I not see this?

It was a hot September day and we had previously brought mums bed downstairs to the front room as she was already having trouble getting up and down the stairs. On this day she was walking from her chair across the room to her bed and she had a fall. She was taken to hospital and an x-ray showed she had broken her hip and would need surgery, so she was admitted straight away for an emergency operation.

My mother's anxieties made her fear hospitals and doctors and in her later years no matter how ill or unwell she felt, she would never seek a doctor's advice. However this had all happened so quickly and was beyond her control. It was agreed she would have to have a hip replacement to allow her to walk again and the operation and what it entailed all seemed to go well.

A few days later two carers got my mum out of bed to use the commode, "Come on Mrs

Arnold." I heard one nurse say, "You should be able to stand now." Both nurses stood each side of my mother, I could just see beneath the privacy curtain my mum's small feet in her slippers shuffling, trying to get to her commode, while the nurses talked over her, quite happily chatting about other things going on that day, they didn't seem to hear my mother's voice.

"It hurts," I heard my mum repeat. I felt so helpless. Should I rush in and help, were they right, should she be able to stand on it by day three? I still don't know the answers to this day, but before I could think any more on the subject I was aware of my mum's deafening scream as she had fallen hard landing on her hip yet again, re opening part of a massive hip wound of around 7 inches.

Manic scenes followed with nurses rushing to lift my poor mother back to her bed, followed by doctors being called. She was taken back to theatre but they were unable to re stitch the wound. So in the days that followed, my mum was taken to theatre every day so they could clean and re-dress her wound hoping it would heal itself over time and allowing her skin to re-join. This never happened however and over the next few weeks I was becoming very aware that it had started to have a nasty distinctive odour. I mentioned this many times to the nurse in charge, but was always reassured that all was going well and that the hospital and Doctor's where doing as much as they could to help my mum.

I remember visiting my mother the night before she died on October 23rd 1997. I parked the car and started to run across the car park to get a parking ticket. It was a cold, wet and windy evening and I could feel the cold rain smacking against my hot cheeks as I searched my purse for the right money. I had come straight from ASDA where I had finished my shift at 8 o'clock and just wanted to say goodnight to my mum before going home. I still had my ASDA uniform on and hadn't brought a coat as the weather in the afternoon had been sunny when I had left home.

My mother looked pale and very vulnerable as I walked in to her private room which had been given to her since her fall. She certainly had lost weight in the four weeks she had been in hospital and this had become so apparent now as I looked at her tiny body in what seemed like an oversized hospital bed.

"Hello sweetheart," she said as she slowly turned her head, catching sight of my presence.

"I won't kiss you mum," I said, trying to lighten the mood, "I'm soaked and freezing."

"At home in my wardrobe in the front spare bedroom I have a lovely coat that will fit you, have it," she whispered.

I laughed and said. "Don't be silly mum what are you going to wear when you get home?"

She looked very calmly at me and said, "I'm not coming home Steph."

I joked and laughed again. "Why, where you going?" I asked, trying to lift the mood again.

"I'm dying." she said.

However cold I was feeling this was nothing like the ice cold chill that I had just felt run through my body.

I told myself not to be so silly. I would know and I have had no feelings or premonition of this, so that has to be a good sign.

I took her hand and said, "Mum, please don't worry, it's your anxieties taking hold again, people don't die of a broken hip."

She gently looked back and said. "No one can feel as ill as this and come through it Stephanie."

"Don't be silly," I told her.

Later after visiting for about an hour I could see mum was becoming very tired and needed to sleep, so I quietly picked up my chair to move it back against the wall where I had got it, away from her bed. I crept slowly to the ward door I gently turned the handle trying not to wake her. As I turned for a last goodbye glance, mum raised her hand in a wave. I told her I would see her tomorrow afternoon and hopefully she would be feeling a bit better, but for now she must sleep.

The next day was a Friday, 24th October, the sun was shining, and it was a much better day then the cold chilly night before. So I made a plan in my head, I will enjoy this day and walk my dog in the afternoon to enjoy the sun, then I will go to work and do my three hour shift and when I am finished I will pop and see mum like I had done the night before.

I told myself that she wouldn't mind, she would know I will visit at some point. So I did, I walked my dog along the woods in the beautiful sunshine, catching the light and the warmth as it escaped through the trees to make shadows and reflections on the earth beneath me. I will tell mum about this walk and promise her that when she feels better I will bring her to show her this beautiful place.

After about an hour I arrived home and got ready for work. I arrived at ASDA at 4.30pm, this would give me time to have a quick coffee before I start work at 5pm I told myself, feeling quite proud of how I had planned my day out.

"Telephone call for Stephanie Carr," was the voice that caught my ear over the loud tannoy.

"Did they just call me?" I asked the young girl I was sitting sharing my coffee with.

"Wasn't listening," she replied with a chuckle.

"Oh well if it's important they will call again," I muttered, "I shouldn't even be here yet anyway."

Within minutes came the second call over the tannoy, this time the receptionist had an urgent quite abrupt sound to her voice.

"Would Stephanie Carr please call reception? Urgent!"

My heart started to thump in my chest, with a hundred and one things with what could have gone wrong in the forty minutes that had passed since I had left home.

I picked up the phone in the canteen and dialled reception.

"It's Stephanie," I said and yet again I could hear the shakiness in my voice.

I have your husband on the phone Steph said the receptionist.

"I'm in the canteen, put him through please."

"What's up?" I spurted as soon as I heard his voice say "Steph."

"You should go to the hospital," he insisted Oh was that all he wanted to tell me? I felt my body relax down as I presided to reassure him, "I am going after my shift at 8pm," I replied. "I'm not, not going, I just decided to walk the dog this afternoon because the sun was out and thought I would go tonight."

"You should go now!" he insisted, "The hospital has just called for you."

I left the building within seconds of that phone call, not even telling a single person that

I would not be in for work and that my shift would need covering. There was no importance in my head other than the one that I needed to get to my mum and now! The Friday night traffic was a nightmare and it seemed to take forever to get from one side of town to the other.

I arrived at the hospital around 5.45pm and by this time my mother had already slipped in to a coma.

Oh no I thought, what if I had only kept my word and visited this afternoon, maybe I could have seen something was wrong, maybe I would have been able to sit and talk to her one last time. Then my mind was taken to the conversation we had had the night before, when she had tried to tell me she was dying. Did she know and was trying to tell me? Why? I shouted to anyone who wanted to listen. "Why if I can see and sense things did you not show me and prepare me for this?!" I felt very let down and angry.

Mum passed at 6.55pm that night, with all her children around her bed.

We later learnt that because of mum's fall she had contracted the MRSA virus. I wondered if this was responsible for the bad odour around my mum. This had just been shrugged off when mentioned many times to medical staff. This in turn had caused septicaemia. The cause of mum's death, a perforated colon brought on by the above.

The night after mum passed my sister and I went to mum's house, which was still our old family home. The outside light was always left on, night and day, mum would never turn it off as she said that if she did, "She would forget to turn it on and people would trip over the front door step." As we both stood on the step my sister searching in her bag for mum's house keys, the light just went out all on its own! Just like the landing light had gone out straight after dad had passed. My sister and I smiled at each other, "That's mum's little sign, the same sign as dad showed us that all was well when he passed." I said, my sister agreed.

After a lot of soul searching and as time has passed, I have learnt that even being spiritual and having insight in things does not protect me from the pain and hurt in this life. I, just like anyone else, have to experience these things. I do not have any 'given right' to be shielded from them, as it is a part of my souls growth to endure, learn and grow from these lessons. I have become even more aware that my gift is there to help others and that I cannot or should not have any emotional personal gain from it. My gift is there merely to bring, love, peace, reassurance and guidance to the sad, lost and suffering. I should expect no right to be cushioned by any power or insight I may have, I am, after all, just a normal person leading a normal life.

At the time of my mum's passing I was just starting out as a medium, the more evenings I did for the church, the more people were asking for my help and to see me.

When my youngest Joshua was about to go to high school I could do this and work from home.

I had never wanted to make a self-financial gain from my work but I was finding it very difficult to hold down my job at ASDA and manage the demand from people wanting my help. One of them would have to give.

After discussing this with my husband, I decided to give up work and put my energy whole heartedly in to helping others. I had always decided the large group events I took on would always be on a charity basis, this way, in my mind I couldn't be seen to be doing any wrong. Yet again my upbringing, Bible quotes and self-doubts were still lurking in my subconsciousness. But if, through my gift, I was helping to raise money and awareness for people far less fortunate then myself, well then I would sit very happily with that. Maybe that's why I had been born with this gift in the first place? I would however have to cover the cost of the money I would be losing from giving up my job. So my plan was to do six readings a week, plus any charity events that I was asked to do. The readings done at home would cover the pay I would be losing from work. I could never try and do any more than this, as after most readings I am left with a headache and feeling somewhat drained. Also I would have to limit my charity events to two or three a month, as I always wake up the morning after an event with a banging migraine that can last up to six hours at a time.

So this is what happened and over the next few years I became very well known in my town and up and down the country through my work. I am also very proud that to date I have probably raised thousands of pounds for many different local charities over the years. This is my pride in life and my own stamp that I have helped to make a difference with the tools I was born with.

A Night I Won't Forget

I was asked to do a charity event in Felixstowe in Suffolk. The lady who had asked me to do this was trying to raise money for Ipswich Hospice, where she had recently lost her father. I, as always, agreed and turned up on July 6th 2005.

I remember arriving on what was a very warm sunny evening. The evening was being held in the events room at a local hotel in Felixstowe and around two hundred people had turned up to support this function. I had a few smiles from strangers as I was welcomed and walked through the hall to set my PA system up.

As the evening started the hall which had been full of laughter and chit chat fell silent as all eyes were fully focused on me waiting for me to begin.

Straight away as I closed my eyes I saw the word "Aldgate". Nothing more followed it, but the sense I was feeling was fear and sickness.

"Can anyone take Aldgate?" I asked. (When I say 'take', it is when I give a word or a name and I am asking if it has relevance or meaning to anyone). Not one person raised their hand.

"I have no idea why I am seeing this word but it comes with the feeling of fear and upset."

I searched the room, but again not one person put their hand up. So for now I had no choice but to let it go and carry on with another message.

Half way through the evening, again and even stronger this time I saw the word again, ALDGATE. This time I thought I was going to be physically sick right on the spot and I felt more than one person's passing.

"Someone must be able to take this." I pleaded, "As this is now making me feel quite unwell."

Still no one raised their hand, so for the second time that night, I let the message go.

As the night went on I kept seeing the number 30 flash before my eyes, again along with this feeling of sickness, again when offering to see if anyone knew why I would be feeling and seeing this, not one person raised their hand… and I was becoming very aware of the frustration now being felt by people, so allowed the message to go and tried to carry on with my evening.

The next morning I awoke with the usual migraine from working the night before. I had just taken the migraine pill, accompanied by a cup of weak tea when my phone started to ring. I answered it and it was the lady who had organised the event the night before.

"Stephanie!" she shouted with what could only be described as complete shock in her voice. "Have you seen the news?"

"No, I've only just woken up, what's up?"

"You know you kept saying Aldgate last night, well Aldgate Tube Station has been bombed this morning with multiple deaths!"

My hand clasped the phone and a cold sweat and wave of sickness came over my whole body. I stood in silence trying to recall anything else I may have felt or seen last night.

"I'm really worried that the Police are going to think you had something to do with it, as you mentioned it in front all of those people last night."

I laughed, "Just because I have insight doesn't make me guilty of the crime." I answered, plus I had had no real detail or proof to follow this up with, just the name, Aldgate, and the fear and sickness that followed.

"It is very frustrating for me at times." I told her. "

Many more phone calls through out that day followed, all with shock from people who had attended the event only a few hours before.

I only wish that if I had been given more detail or insight I may have been able to go to the police with some kind of warning. But yet again, who is to say they would have taken me seriously or even believed me.

Sonia Mayes organiser of the Hospice Charity Event testimonial

"After losing my dad to cancer in 2004 I turned to Stephanie for some guidance. I had been doing a lot of charity work for the hospice as they were amazing with my dad until the end and I wanted to give something back. I decided to ask Stephanie to do a clairvoyant night for me in which she very kindly agreed.

The event was a sell-out straight away and on the night the messages came flowing through. Towards the end of the first half, Steph asked if anyone could take the name Aldgate Road, place, station or anywhere with Aldgate in it. No-one could take it so she moved on. In the second half it came up again, Aldgate, also the number 30, again no-one could take the message.

The night came to a close and we had a chat at the end where she said she couldn't get Aldgate out of her head and it wasn't good. Thinking no more of it I went home extremely happy as we had raised £1300!

The following day I was listening to the news and heard that there had been a bombing in London. As I watched the news they said that Aldgate Station had been bombed. I went cold and had to phone Steph! I said "I'm in a state of shock have you seen the news?"

She said no, but was then putting the news on.

She said that she had just put her telly on and could see the news and it all made sense from the night before!

Rather flippantly I said that I hope the police don't come looking for her!

After our conversation the news went on to report that a bus had also been bombed as well. Yep, you guessed it, number 30!"

Beggars Belief!

I remember one morning…

I was busy hanging washing out in the garden when I thought I could hear my phone ringing back inside the house. I quickly ran inside to answer it before my answer machine kicked in.

"Is that Stephanie?" was the first thing I heard as I picked up the phone.

It came from a very well-spoken lady on the other end.

"Yes it is." I replied. "Can I help you?"

"I really hope so." she said and with that I heard the sigh and drop in her voice as she took a breath before she continued.

"I think I have something nasty like a spirit in my home, would you come and see please?"

Until this date, I had never become involved with anything of a "dark nature" from the other side and in all honesty I had no idea what I would be dealing with or what I may be letting myself in for or my family. But I was somewhat blasé and very naïve about the whole subject, and found myself instantly saying. "Yes of course I will."

Not wanting to go to this house alone I called on two friends to come along with me, Myra and David. I had met both at Horley Spiritual Church and they were both spiritual healers and like minded people who were well aware of the afterlife. They themselves had also been called to a few homes in the past when the owner had reported that they thought they had a spirit or presence living with them. I, however, had not. How hard can this be? What could possibly happen to me? Just go to the house and see what I feel, that is all that had been asked of me, so that is all I have to do. I told myself and that was my only plan.

It was early evening when we arrived at the property. It was quite hard to find as all there was from the main road was a dusty old dirt track that went on for around a quarter of a mile before it eventually led us to the foot of a beautiful looking house. Everything from the windows to the roof was just stunning to look at and as I got out from the car and walked up to the massive archway that led us to the front door. I was in awe of this beautiful house and the person who was lucky enough to be living there.

I knocked on the large solid wood door, and took a few steps back, again taking another gaze over the house.

What caught my eye was, *"Built in 1621"* written within the brickwork across the large front door.

The door quickly opened and before us stood a tall slim, very well spoken lady.

"Hello," she said, with a big smile. Her friendly nature put me at ease and removed any apprehension I may have felt about going.

"Come in," she insisted.

As we walked through the giant front door it led onto the dining room. This home was just as beautiful inside as it was from the outside and I could feel that my mouth and jaw seemed to be wide open in amazement as to what I was seeing. In their dining room stood the longest table I had ever seen which was made from thick solid dark oak which could comfortably seat around twenty people.

"Would you like me to show you around?" The owner of this house asked.

"Yes please," I replied. "I have to say that I am not feeling anything nasty or dark here, you have a beautiful home." She smiled, a somewhat nervous smile as she led me through a smaller door compared to the rest of the house, which opened up to their lounge.

"Wow," I said in disbelief.

The stone fireplace was the main feature of the whole side of the room and took up an entire wall! It was so big you could literally walk into it! There were stacks of freshly cut logs all neatly placed around it ready for the cold evenings. Each room, the lounge and dining room had wooden patio doors that led out to acres of beautifully kept garden. The furniture was in character with the house. Whoever this lady and her family were, they certainly had some money and came from riches to own such a property.

We were then led to the other side of the house and into the kitchen. "And this is the kitchen." she said as she walked over to the double stove to fill the kettle ready to offer us all a drink after showing us around. The kitchen was just as grand and this was the main focus of the house with fruit and veg sitting on the table ready to be prepared for the next meal. There were dishes stacked on the draining board after what would have been a heavy dinner for the family. As my eyes scanned this room I was taken back to the corner of the kitchen where a set of around five steps led down to a small door. "What's in there? I asked.

"That's the cellar," she replied. "Would you like to go in and take a look?"

"No thanks," Was my response which spontaneously came straight out of my mouth.

This was the first time since entering this house my senses had been awakened, but I had no idea why at this point.

David, the guy who had come along with Myra and I jumped at the chance. "Yes please I would like to look."

"He only wants to see if there is any alcohol stored in there" I joked to Myra, trying to make light of the situation. By now I had a growing feeling of apprehension as I looked at the door. Myra was a dear friend who I trusted and looked up to dearly, she is also very like myself with her outlook on wanting to help others and her healing over the years had helped so many people. I was very lucky and glad that she had also kindly agreed to come with us today.

"I don't like the feeling from down there." David said as he rejoined us.

"Why did it not have any wine?" I joked.

We were then led up the stairs by a steep stairway which led out to a very narrow hallway. We were shown into the first double bedroom where stood a large four poster bed. The two small paned windows looked out onto open fields. Oh my, fancy waking up in this room with this view.

As I turned to exit back onto the hallway still in awe of this fabulous house I presided to walk along a seemingly sloping floor and there it happened! I had a feeling that was so native to me. In an instant, it was as if I had stepped right into a freezer, every hair on my body stood up! The air had gone ice cold! Even so, I could feel the sweat in my arm pits, on the back of my neck and the palms of my hands, my senses instantly come to life.

I felt fear! And I mean real fear!

Everything, every sense that I had, told me to get out now!

The lady of the house instantly noticed the change in me, as if she had been waiting to see if it would happen. "You feel it don't you?" she asked.

"I do," I replied. "I really have to go as I am feeling a bit of an upset tummy coming on."

"Please stay for a cup of tea," she insisted, "I have popped the kettle on already."

"I must go," I urged Myra and David as they had also sensed my eagerness to get away as quickly as I could.

I got in the car and as David started to drive back down the stony dusty dirt track he glanced over to me, "You okay?"

"Don't ever take me back to that house again," I blurted.

That was it, I promised myself that I would never ever do work like this again.

They smiled at each other as they had both been to many properties before and experienced things of a dark nature so this wasn't impacting on them as much as it was for me.

I was the first one to be dropped off home and I thanked them both for coming with me. How would I have coped if I had gone alone I wondered as I closed the car door, and waved goodbye.

"How was it?" Tim asked as I walked in.

"Well I won't be doing that again." I said, "It was horrible and I still feel a little sick."

I soon settled that evening, now back in my own home and with the safety of my own surroundings.

That night after going to bed, I fell in to such a deep sleep. In this sleep I dreamt I was back at the old 1621 house, it looked a little different, much older this time. There where children in the house, lots of children, scrubbing floors and cleaning and cooking. All the children were very fearful, pale looking, and extremely thin. In the dream I walked in to the kitchen towards the cellar door and came face to face with a man in a white coat, his was not a friendly face and I could see he was doing some kind of experiments on some of the children. One child had his Achilles tendon cut so he was unable to run away, while others sat cowering in the corner. The smell, even in this dream was horrific. The man turned and looked me right in the eye and shouted at me to leave his house and never return! I woke up with a gasp! The feeling I had was the same I experienced a few hours earlier, the sweat was pouring off me and I was so very scared.

Tim woke up straight away feeling my panic and asked if I was okay? I told him of my dream.

"You don't need to ever go back there, try and clear your mind of it and relax," he urged.

I looked over to the clock, it was 3am and this is known to some as the witching hour being the opposite of 3pm when Jesus was crucified which highlights the good and bad in us all.

When I awoke later everything didn't seem quite so bad and I pushed my dream and the happenings of the day before out of my mind. About an hour or so after I had got up the phone rang. "Hello." said that quiet but very polite voice and I was instantly aware that it was the lady from the house.

"I'm just calling to see if you're okay as you hurried off so quickly last night and I was worried about you."

"Oh I'm fine, I did feel something, but I don't know enough to be able to help you I'm afraid or even really want to. I also had a nasty dream last night." I found myself explaining to her what I had seen and dreamt. She took a big sigh and then said. "I have done some investigation and the gentleman who built this house was from London and held a high position within the church. After he died the house was handed down to his son who wanted to be a doctor in medicine. He used to take the poor and beggar children in, offering work for small handouts of food and it is said that some children was never seen again!"

Oh my God! I thought, so the things I had seen in my dream seemed to be correct.

"I am sorry I can't help you any more with this." I found myself explaining now wanting to hurriedly get off the phone.

I made myself a drink, and sat down. What was this all about? I asked myself. And how have I got myself so involved emotionally?

I phoned Myra and explained what had happened. "Come and see me now, you need healing, you need to cut cords with this place emotionally and we need to put some protection around you."

I didn't have to be invited twice and I jumped at the chance of her offer.

Myra completed her healing in her beautiful healing spiritual room which filled me with instant peace and calm on entering it, the room was filled with gold angel ornaments and crystals, with a sweet yet non over powering gentle smell surrounding it. Within her room she has all of her certificates hanging on the wall showing all the achievements this lady has gained and the knowledge of mind, spirit and body techniques. The healing was lovely and I felt assured that I was now protected against anything dark.

I came home much happier and continued my day.

I had of course briefly explained about the house to Tim and he was aware of my dream the night before, but I had not or would not discuss these things with my children. I did not wish for them to know too much about my work until they were old enough to understand. They could then make up their own mind about religion and choose the pathway they felt was right for them to follow.

That night I went to bed and had a very good sleep. I woke at around five am as I heard Tim shut the front door behind him as he left for work. I felt very relieved that I hadn't had a bad dream again and Myra's healing had worked so I quietly drifted back off to sleep. I was awoken about an hour later with a scream from my daughter's bedroom, she was thirteen at the time. I jumped out of bed and rushed as quickly as I could to her room. "Mum." she said. "I had the most awful dream that I was in this really old house, and this man wanted to hurt me. I couldn't get away and there were other frightened children there also. We were being picked as we were led into a dark room under the house where he wanted to take our skin off our backs to reuse and stitch back on again. You were standing there mum and this horrible man in a white coat was shouting at me, to tell you, to keep away!"

I froze. How I wasn't physically sick on the spot I will never know. How had this energy managed to get into my daughter's and my head? I, as a mother wanted to reassure her it was just a dream and nothing like that would happen to her. But I was also fearful in what I had opened myself and my family up to. This was far from just a dream.

I had let Myra put protection around me so he could not penetrate my mind and thoughts but we had both overlooked to protect the people who were close to me, or my home. He was able to use my daughter's thoughts and mind to yet again warn me to keep away!

As soon as it started to become light I phoned Myra explaining what had happened and Lucy's dream. Her advice was. "You need to confront this now, no more running away from it, if he can use your children in this way he needs to be stopped and fast!

"But how do I do that?" I asked.

"The first thing is to find out where he is laid to rest."

"Ok I will call the lady as she told me she had done some research on the history of the house."

Myra said that she would ask for and send protection to all my family and home.

I immediately phoned the lady and she was quite surprised to hear from me.

"I wonder if I can ask you something." I could hear the nervousness in my own voice, quite different from the first time we spoke. "The gentleman that wanted to be a doctor you spoke about who lived in the house?"

"Yes," she replied.

"Do you know where he was laid to rest?"

"Yes," she said and proceeded to tell me the name and address of the cemetery. I then called David and asked if he would come and look for this man's grave and head stone, that's if he even had one. He agreed and later that day we took off looking around every stone in the grave yard. Luckily for us the grave yard was in a small village so there weren't too many stones to look through which was good

95

as we only had a name to go on. David had come prepared with his wire brush which he needed to use to clean most of the moss that had grown over the old head stones allowing us to read any inscription written on them.

After hours of looking we found nothing. "It might be one of the old stones we can't read," he said. "Or he may not even have a headstone."

I left feeling very vulnerable and disappointed at not being able to find what I had set out for. That night I had another dream. I was standing in the grave yard alone and as I looked at all the stones I was told to walk toward the church, as I approached it a hand came out from under the church wall, reaching out to me!

I woke again with a start. Sitting up with sweat once again running down my face. I looked over at the clock, it was 3am once again. I quietly got out of bed and went to check in on Lucy who was fast asleep and peaceful. Thank God it was my dream. I said inwardly.

I went back to bed, and after what seemed an age I drifted off to sleep again.

The next day I phoned the lady again. "I'm really sorry to trouble you but I couldn't find any trace of him in the church yard do you have any idea where in the churchyard he may be?

"I don't," she replied. "But I am sure if you ask the vicar he might know."

So that day David and I went searching again. I found the address of the vicar of the church and before I could give it any thought I was standing at the rectory knocking on the door. The vicar answered and with a kind smile asked if he could help me.

"I am doing some history on a 17th century house," I explained. "I believe the man that lived in the house is buried in your church yard and I wonder if you had any idea where he is positioned." Okay it was a little white lie. But I was hardly going to tell him the truth and I was doing some historical research, in a way.

I gave him the name. "Oh yes!" he replied.

"I know where he is buried but he is not in the church yard though, he is buried inside the church."

Oh my, that is why I saw the hand reaching out from underneath the wall of the church in my dream last night. I have since been told that back in pagan and Christianity times it is said that if you were rich or came from high status you could ensure your body could be buried in the church itself, giving you assurance that nothing bad would become of your remains. It was also believed that people who were bad and didn't deserve such a funeral would also be buried at night in secret.

David and I took ourselves, yet again, back to the cemetery and this time with the loan of the key from the vicar for an hour we were able to go inside the church.

We found where this man was laid to rest, he was to the side of the main alter at the front of the church. I sat on the front seat of the church and I prayed like I had never prayed before, for peace for him and all he had done in this world. For peace to all the children and people whose life had been affected by him. For peace and protection to myself and my family and home. I then slowly walked over and, along with David, rested our hands on the stone that had an inscription of this man's life.

I said out loud in the church that I was sorry for ever going in to his home and wished him peace and love. I said I had no evil in me, only love and if he wanted to take any part of me, he would be taking good and love, which I freely offered. As I stood up, the imprint of sweat of both our hands remained for what seemed an age on this cold pale stone. We locked the church back up and walked away.

Very soon after this I was told the lady had people in to clear and bless the house, and shortly after that moved away.

To date I have never had another dream regarding this, nor has Lucy. I will never open myself up or work with any kind of dark energy like this ever again.

Visions and Premonitions

This is where my senses of sight, sound and feelings become heightened beyond my control.

Premonition no: 1

Road Traffic Accident

I remember a day a few years back. I had pulled a muscle in my back quite badly and was off work. I was offered some private physiotherapy but it meant I had to drive to Woodbridge to receive it, which is about 10 miles from where I live.

Any offers of help to get me back on my feet and mobile again were greatly received.

It was a lovely sunny autumn day, and I was travelling along the A12 towards Woodbridge. I remember at the time I had the local radio on, and it was playing a Kylie Minogue song so I had the volume turned up a little higher than usual, the window was open and yes I admit I was singing at the top of my voice. I approached a roundabout and midway around it I heard, what sounded like the loudest truck horn! I looked to my right to see a massive American-like lorry coming straight towards me!

The horn sounded like one of those horns you pull, like on films and the noise seem to go on continuously. I really thought this is it, this lorry is going to hit me. Before I had time to breathe or think, I was pulling away from the roundabout. God that was close I thought with a gasp, and I could still feel my heart pounding and my hands sweating as I gripped the steering wheel. But as I looked back in my mirror, I could see nothing, no sign at all of a lorry. I pulled over at the nearest petrol station and got out of my car. What an earth happened there? How can a lorry that big just disappear? Still feeling very shaky I returned to my car and continued my journey for my 2pm appointment, feeling shook up but very lucky to still be alive.

When I returned home around 3.30pm I told Tim what had happened.

"You sure there was no lorry?" Tim asked.

"It would have been too big to just vanish!" I replied. "But that's just what it did."

Around 5.45 that evening Tim was in the kitchen when he called me to him. "Listen to the news on the radio." he said.

I stood silently as I leaned up against the worktop giving my back some support, I heard the reporter as he spoke informing people that the A12 at Woodbridge roundabout was closed, due to a fatality between a car and a lorry that had happen around 5pm.

Was what I saw at the very same spot three hours earlier a premonition? I asked myself. To this day I still have no answers to my question. But I do know that what I saw and felt was very real to me. However, the feeling of having a premonition where I could see and feel so clearly but also being totally powerless to do absolutely anything to prevent, became very frustrating to me.

Premonition no: 2

Watch the back of your car

The next time something similar to this happened I was again driving. This time it was around 10pm and in the dark. As I drove along a winding country lane I had a quick flash in my mind of my husband's friend Greg. Straight after I thought of him I saw a quick vision of his car being hit around one of the rear wheels. The vision was very quick and brief, but again the feeling that came with it felt very real. I arrived home around 10.30pm and Tim was dozing in the chair. "You have to ring Greg!" I spurted out as I walked in to the lounge.

"What! Why?" he said, coming out of a gentle sleep.

I could see the confusion sweep over his face at being woken up so abruptly.

"I just saw his car get hit," I shouted.

Greg is a lovely family friend, who works as a bank manager, so drives very classy expensive cars, but is also the most down to earth family oriented person you could ever wish to meet.

"I'm not calling him now Stephanie, the poor guy will most probably be in bed asleep Tim shouted. At that moment and for a brief second I felt the same reaction I used to get as a child, of not being believed and being told to be quiet. "You just can't come out with things like that Stephanie."

Mum's words again coming flooding back to me.

But I was stronger now, and more persistent. I also had come to trust my feelings, so was not prepared to let this go. "Okay," I replied to Tim in annoyance. "But you must call him first thing tomorrow."

We went off to bed and as soon as I felt him start to get up the next morning I was on at him again. "Please Tim, please call Greg."

"And say what?!" came his abrupt answer, "That he's going to be hit in his car? Come on Steph, you can't go round frightening people like that."

"I know but if I have seen this and me telling him prevents it from happening then we have to. What if we don't tell him, and something bad happens, would we, could we be able to forgive ourselves? Please Tim," I begged. "Make the call."

So around 7.30am I heard Tim call Greg, the usual chit chat went on, with the how are you mate. Then I heard Tim's voice become more serious. "Steph has been nagging me to call you, you know she gets messages and sees things," he said. "Last night she said she saw you, and your car got hit on the rear drivers' side wheel."

Tim said that Greg replied, "Really? Well it's not happened yet." He assured him and a little chuckle between them both gave way to any awkwardness that may have been felt from this conversation even having to be taken.

"There done! Now stop worrying and let it go." he said when he came off the telephone.

I have since been told that Greg came off the phone to Tim and told his wife what I had seen.

"Shall I drive into London today?" he asked her.

"Well Greg, this is your job and you can't stop going into work because of a vision. Just check your back wheels before you leave and drive safely," she advised.

That evening on Greg's return driving back from London his car was clipped by an articulated lorry on his right back wheel. He was not hurt, but just a little shook up by the whole episode.

Since this happened Greg always listens to me now, avidly!

Premonition no: 3

Transition from body form to spirit

It was Christmas Day 2004. My dear father- in- law Ken had been diagnosed with bowel cancer in the January, 11 months earlier and was losing his battle, after receiving all the treatment the hospital could offer.

It had been a somewhat hectic day, as you can imagine, with three children and an early start. Tim had been staying with his parents for two weeks as his father was by this time very ill. Tim came home to have Christmas dinner with myself and our children, only staying an hour or so before returning back to his parents taking a Christmas dinner for his mum. Myself and the children planned to go round and join him later that afternoon. His father had spent around the last six weeks bed-ridden and was very weak and was nearing the end however he was peaceful and was comatose. He always enjoyed seeing his grandchildren, even if it was for a quick hello and cuddle.

After clearing the dishes and the mess from Christmas dinner I set off with the kids around mid-afternoon.

My father-in-law was very weak and the children weren't able to see him. I sat quietly with him. We didn't stay too long and the children were getting restless, so I decided to set off home taking them with me. Tim was staying with his mother as he didn't want to leave her alone, so he decided to stay a little longer and planned to rejoin me at home later.

I came home and if I'm honest, just sat straight down. I was getting myself ready and very much looking forward to an hours viewing of EastEnders and Coronation Street. It was in the second "soap" and around 8.30pm when as clear as day I saw my father- in-law Ken standing in my lounge! There was no expression on his face at all and he was wearing a green sweat shirt.

At the very same moment my son Aaron who was 15 at the time came running in from the kitchen and said, "Mum I just saw granddad standing in the kitchen wearing a green sweatshirt."

How could he show himself in two different places but in the same house? I asked myself.

I quickly phoned my husband on his mobile.

"Tim has your dad passed? Both Aaron and I just saw him here very clearly!"

"I don't think so," he said, "But I am downstairs. I'll go and have a look."

I stayed on the phone as I heard him climb the stairs to go and check on his father.

"No, he is still with us, but his breathing has changed and much slower and spaced out, I think you should come back."

I quickly told the children I had to pop back to grandmas to pick dad up, and left Aaron in charge, he never minded this, and quite like being left with authority over his sister and brother.

I arrived back at Tim's parents' house around 15 minutes after our phone call and his father had just passed away.

It is my belief that the few hours just before you pass and your breathing becomes very slow and intermittent with long gaps between breaths that our spirit can travel in and out of

109

our body. I believe that my father-in-law made a visit to his grandchildren before leaving this planet.

On returning home that night and as we walked in our house, I turned our hall light on, only for the bulb to blow!

The uncanny sign always shown to me that all was well.

The Best Conversation I Ever Had After a Charity Event

I wanted to include and share something that meant more to me than I can ever put into words.

After mum had passed I was holding another charity function, at Horley Spiritual Church. The hall was once again packed with around one hundred and twenty people. The night was being held by a lady who was battling breast cancer, and wanted to raise funds for Somersham ward at Ipswich Heath Road hospital. To my amazement at the end of the evening a lady and her daughter approached me. It was the same lady that had lived at the house adjoining my back garden as a child and her daughter was my childhood friend. "Oh Aunty Brenda how lovely to see you." I said, as I gently gave them both a hug, feeling very surprised that they had even bothered to come and watch me.

"Your mother told me," she said.

"Told you?" I replied, with a look of not having the foggiest idea what she was talking about.

"When you were a little girl and I lost my husband Charlie, remember?" I nodded. "Yes of course I do."

"Your mother came to my house and told me that you had seen him in our garden. It gave us as a family so much comfort, at the time. She said how much she felt you had something a little different about you, but as your mother, she also wanted to protect you from any ridicule."

I felt happiness, sadness and numbness all together at the same moment. Mum never told me she did this. Of all the times I thought mum wasn't listening, or didn't believe me, she was just trying to protect me. She had believed me enough to put herself out and even be laughed at by passing my message on for me to this lovely family.

Thank you mum x

Over the years seeing and feeling things have become a very big part of my life, like plane crashes and terrorist attacks along with the earth's vibrations and volcanoes. I have no idea why I see or sense such things when I have no power to stop or prevent them from happening and I find it all terribly frustrating.

On drawing my book to a close, I now do more and more charity functions and to date have helped raised thousands of pounds for many different well known good causes. Some Christian people or other religious faiths will say I am doing the work of the devil. But I do not believe that raising money for charity and bringing love and light to people in need is anything close to the devil's work. Plus my heart is filled with too much love. Every night is different and every event brings people closer to opening their mind up to something more, way beyond just the physical we see. To me it is like air, we can't see it, or hold it, but nevertheless, it's there, and we wouldn't survive without it.

Every event leaves me the next morning waking to a migraine and feeling drained, but this is a small price to pay to being able to bring people closer to loved ones they have lost, bridging the gap and bringing proof, peace and reassurance in whatever way I can.

Testimonials

I would like to take this opportunity to thank everyone who has given me permission to share their experience in providing so much detail of what, for them, was a very emotional and difficult time.

I look forward to writing and sharing my second book with you in time

Wishing love, light and happiness to you all.

"Hello! How to describe the utter mind blowing experience of my first meeting with Stephanie Carr! I was on holiday when I received a text saying a fund-raiser was being organised and Stephanie Carr was hosting a Clairvoyant evening. I have friends who have been to lots and had private readings but it has never been something I have thought of or believed in. However I said I would have two tickets, not intending to attend but to donate the entrance fee anyway. So finding myself queueing up to be seated with my close friend and 150 others was a surprise, but there I was.

Stephanie was a petite lady who sat quietly on her own at the front and when the first message came through it was quickly taken by someone who seemed to genuinely take comfort and reassurance from the words given to her. Before the interval Stephanie asked if there were any real sceptics in the room I had to be honest and raised my hand not expecting to be called up but Stephanie asked if I would like to go forward and urged on by my friend I stepped up and sat down with Stephanie to my right. She took two very large breaths and said, "Your Mum is very pleased you got the ring."

Now my mum had been dead for just over two years and with some of my inheritance I purchased a very large diamond solitaire. Now you may say that most daughters would get a ring from their mother so no huge spine tingle there but the fact that my dear Mum had passed and I bought a ring" OK. "Your Mum says that her day was so beautiful and she is very proud of you, although you knew it would all be down to you."

So, it was a spectacular funeral, even if I do say so myself and my brother and Mum's partner had left it all to me, every last detail and I had been praised by so many people for the beautifully touching service. I must say I was starting to just believe when Stephanie came up with her trump card. "Your mum wants to know why she doesn't have a headstone?"

Now she had me hook line and sinker!

Mums ashes are in a cupboard in my dining room. I just couldn't bear to part with them. Now, there is just no way, no way at all that you could guess this, which you could talk around anything other than some way, somehow, this amazing lady was able to convey messages from my darling Mum. The intention was to bury them with my Dad but I just hadn't got the strength to go that final step.

"She knows it's hard for you but when you know the time is right then she would like a stone."

It was as if she was there, kind, considerate, but gently letting me know. I believed her and when the next few messages came through I was aware of them but it was all a blur. But when Stephanie said Mum was fading I asked her "Please don't go". So what do I know of Stephanie? She has a gift, a wonderful gift of this I am sure. There is one more question I have for her. Well maybe at my next reading.

Lisa (Ipswich)"

"I have been lucky enough to have been audience to Stephanie Carr on at least four occasions. On one particular evening, both my very best friend and I had arranged to go along to a local charitable fundraising evening. We both sat listening to others' encounters with Steph and enjoying seeing people's reactions to her messages. Then Stephanie started to ask for a person that has recently lost a grandparent in the last few days, to which I raised my hand. I had very recently lost my grandmother whom I had not seen in roughly 12 years. Stephanie automatically started to tell me that my Grandma was so very proud of me and was so happy that I was coming home for her funeral. I had booked my ticket to go home to Hawaii that day. Steph continued to tell me that I had someone in my life "Toby" who was very special and shared the same gift as she has. Toby is my son whom has always been a child who will talk to himself and I often found him reading to someone else when he was very young.

I am a Christian by faith and I truly believe that Stephanie is an angel that has been delivered to aid people in a healing process. The pain and relief I have witnessed on others faces and even felt myself when receiving a message from Steph is awe inspiring. What this wonderful woman can give to others when they are often most vulnerable is very special and I can only hope that she continues to share with us all, her gift sent from heaven above."

"One afternoon in early June last year, my Mum asked me if I wanted to tag along with her to a fundraising psychic night that Stephanie Carr was hosting. I'd never attended a psychic event before and wasn't 100% sure how I even feel about it, but I had nothing to do that evening and I didn't want my Mum to go alone.

We arrived to a much smaller group than expected. Perhaps around 10 people in the small village hall side room as opposed to the usual hundred plus audience that Steph usually works with. Steph advised us that the benefit of being in a smaller group was that we'd be more likely to receive a message, but I still didn't imagine that anything would come through for me.

As she navigated her way through the session, it struck me how specific Steph was with the information in her messages, which is something I hadn't anticipated. Having seen other psychics since the evening with Steph, I've learned that she really is exceptionally precise. She was able to list distinct names, dates, ages, relationships, professions, personal items, room/house descriptions, the manner of death for those on the other side. She's incredibly comprehensive and I've yet to see anyone else rival her level of accuracy.

We were about halfway through the evening when she came to me. She had just finished delivering a message to another member of the group when she simply uttered the word 'America' to the room. My stomach flipped, as just the evening before, I had plucked up the courage to tell my partner that I wanted to go away to America to work as an Au Pair. "America", she said again. "Who here is going to America"? I searched the room for anyone else the 'America' remark may apply to, thinking surely it couldn't be me, but no-one spoke up to claim it. I raised a timid hand and Steph turned to me; "you're going to America to work with children, you've wanted to for a long time and you're going to do it".

I nodded and she proceeded; "it will take a little while but you are absolutely going to get there. You'll be overwhelmed at the beginning, but once you get there you'll feel a sense that you've done the right thing and that you're in the right place, and I can see you staying in America long-term".

The next part was where it got interesting; "after about 6 weeks there'll be some changes, you'll need to leave but you'll still stay in America and I can see you staying there for a long time".

Of course, in that moment I couldn't really make sense of that at all, I feared she meant that I'd have to leave America and return to the UK.

Well, I write this from a bedroom 5,500 miles away from where I first heard Stephanie's reading. I've been in America for four weeks now, and after issues with my current placement, I have just finalised plans to move on to a new one. When I move onto my new placement, it will be almost six weeks to the day since my arrival in the U.S. I had no idea how Steph's prediction could come true but so far, it has in every way.

She told me I'd come to America to work with children which I have.

She told me I'd move on after 6 weeks which I'm going to.

She identified English as my strong subject and told me that I'd find unexpected inspiration in writing. Three months ago my Nana died and I wrote a piece about her which amassed over 110,000 'likes' on Facebook and got published in 3 national newspapers!

I could never have foreseen any of these things for myself but somehow Steph did and if I hadn't heard her words that day, I may not have ever found the courage to undertake this challenge and pursue my dream. She gave me faith in my own journey. It's not to say that I don't have bad days sometimes but I don't ever doubt whether I'm on the right path or not now. I feel more sure of myself than I ever have and I take great comfort in knowing that there's so much more to life than simply what the naked eye sees.

Steph's gift opened my mind to the existence of the energies that surround us and through that I've developed a sense of peace which I've never been able to harness before. For myself and I'm sure for many others, hers is a gift that keeps on giving."

"In March 2005, I lost my husband to cancer, he was 55 years old. We had three children and the youngest was only six years old. We were devastated, lost.

His presence was missed terribly, we were struggling to come to terms with it as a family and individually. I had heard about Stephanie by many people, "she is the best" they all said, "she is spot on" they all said!

I found her number, made contact and booked a reading, the morning of the reading came. As I was getting into the car my eldest daughter asked for a lift, I reluctantly agreed to give her a lift, once in the car she asked where I was going. When I told her she reprimanded me telling me I was wasting my money. I replied that she could come and sit next to me quietly or go on her way to her day. She decided to come, hoping she could tell me *"I told you so"*.

Prior to this I had been arguing with my daughters over some tattoos they had done in memory of their dad. He hated tattoos and so did I.

We arrived at Stephanie's door, this pretty lady greeted us with a sunny smile and she invited us in and after the initial ritual she started the reading. My daughter was sitting next to me and she was wearing a cardigan over her clothes. Her arms were not showing.

I was eagerly listening to Stephanie's every word.

One of the first thing she said was, "Your dad is here and he is saying thank you for the tattoos but you didn't need to get them done so big, something smaller would have been better".

I gulped, looked at my daughter who was by then in floods of tears!

There it was the biggest evidence that it was in fact her beloved daddy who was giving the messages to Stephanie. The reading continued, the details and message was so powerful and touching, details that only my husband would have known. Apologies that my husband made to me through Stephanie were very deep and emotional!

The reading finished and my daughter and I were left feeling enveloped by Love, a very special kind of Love that hugs you like a warm blanket on a freezing night, a Love that brings comfort when you are battered and bruised.

That had been a remarkable experience! My daughter and I cried together in the car, hugging each other with a mixture of happiness and relief, Stephanie had given us a precious gift and we will be forever grateful for that light that came at the right time!"

"Hi Steph, hope you are well, here's my feedback, hope it helps!

I had been friends with Tim, Steph's husband for many years, because of work and then through my husband Martyn. Tim and Steph came to stay with us for a while at our house, the previous time had been very eventful but that's another story!

I had wanted a reading for a while but I was a little sceptical for several reasons. Firstly I had had quite a bit of loss and trauma in my life and although I had not spoken about it to Steph, in fact quite the opposite I felt it was a bit 'obvious'. Also I was a bit intrigued and unsure of the process. Steph herself was a little reluctant as she felt that because she was a friend I would think that the things she picked up on where things I had somehow let 'slip' in conversation. I have to say there were things that could have been obtained that way and there were things that the sceptic in me could think 'well that's obvious'.

I thought that she would talk about my Mum from the start, but she didn't, she spoke about my middle daughter Lauren and yes, things like 'she should get on with her website, were generic lifestyle issues but there were two main comments she made that engendered different emotions within me.

The first was when she mentioned 'the flowers'. As a child when my mother died I was not allowed to go to the funeral, which did cause me issues with closure and grieving and I had no idea where her ashes were scattered. I knew the graveyard but not the specific place. For years I never went and then when Lauren was 14, Martyn my husband took me and as we were looking around my youngest daughter Yasmin said that when I died she would know exactly where I was. Lauren on the other hand was upset by the empty graves where no one visited anymore and therefore on the next visit bought some flowers out of her own money and laid one on as many empty graves as she could.

How the hell did Steph know?

I had never told anyone other than Martyn's Mum who had never met Steph. It made me go extremely cold when she said it. Steph mentioned other things that at the time meant nothing but later after investigation turned out to be true. The final word Steph said to me was, what I realise now, I had unconsciously been waiting for, just as I thought and indeed, she thought she had finished. She said one word 'Alice'. That was my Mum's name and I had never told Steph or Tim that name and to be honest if I was to ask Martyn I suspect he wouldn't know it either! I realised when she said that one word that I was not a sceptic at all and I had been waiting for that one word which brought me a great deal of comfort.

So thank you Steph, it appears you knew me better than I knew myself!
Viv xx France"

"Hi Steph, this is how I felt. Being sceptical I resisted the urge to have a reading for a long time. My first husband had died, leaving me with three troubled daughters, but that was 24 years ago. Steph very quickly picked up on this through making some sort of connection with him. She could not have known these facts regarding my past and how it had affected one daughter in particular. Steph also spoke of my late mum's relationship with me and her inability to show physical affection towards me. Both of these observations and apologies gave me a feeling of relief about the past.

As to the future, well I can only say bang on! Steph predicted a wedding this year and a birth for a daughter who has had difficulties having children. Eight miscarriages and many IVF cycles later my daughter is having her 3rd IVF baby at 40, this year!
What a surprise!

And my youngest is getting married too! Lots of things throughout the reading rang little bells, some didn't but I am keeping an open mind about them.

Many thanks for a little peace of mind.
Marilyn (Ipswich)"

"Our daughter had a cardiac arrest two weeks after giving birth to our first grandchild. What should have been a time of great family celebration soon became every parent's worst nightmare and our reality.

Our precious 23 year old daughter lay in a coma fighting for her life. Her new born was without his mother's milk and the whole family were beyond despair. The critical care team were fighting to keep her stable. But as a family, not knowing where to turn we called upon anyone and everyone, pastors, church goers, social media and Stephanie Carr.

Most people know Stephanie Carr the healer, the medium. What many may not know is Stephanie Carr, the woman, who came to us simply because we asked. There was nothing in it for her, other than to console a family in crisis and offer what support she could. Stephanie made no promises, other than to offer her love. What I didn't anticipate, was that she would bring something out in me that I didn't know existed. Before I knew it, I could feel an energy passing though my body, a sensation I had never felt before and haven't felt since. When it stopped, my comatose daughter lifted her arm, as if to acknowledge me. The peace I felt, will stay with me forever more.

Five months on, our girl still has a long way to go, but our grandson has his mum back. We remain in touch with the clinical team and Stephanie and I have one simple message; "Keep doing what you do Stephanie, we will never forget your positive presence, kindness and pure love."

"Hi Steph, so you asked me to write to you regarding my journey with yourself and what you have told me so here it goes.

My mum, my sister & I all came to you for a reading in 2011. You told my mum someone will be in and out of hospital and it will be something to do with their head. At the time I was going to hospital because I had an allergic reaction to hair bleach so we presumed it was me. You also gave a reading to me and some things I remember. My mum then got diagnosed with a Brain Tumour on New Year's Day 2012. She had been going back and forth to the doctors prior to that but no one would recognise the symptoms. It all happened so fast I booked a reading with you again and it was booked in September you then had a cancellation so I was booked for 29th August 2012. My Mum struggled to beat the brain tumour and we would speak to each other about you as we both strongly believed in after life. I told her as a joke, once, mum if you pass away all I want you to say is *"the after-life is real, after life is real"* and describe what it's like up there, will ya?

So things went downhill and on the 28th August 2012 a day before the reading with yourself, my mum passed away at 10 O'clock. I held her hand and she shrugged it off, the hardest pain I will go through in my life.

I still went to see Steph the next day with a poker face!

And you were AMAZING!

You told me you had a lady who hadn't passed very long and how she was in her forties and how it was to do with her head and she was making you feel dizzy. You then said MUM! I knew she had made it over to the other side and the reassurance you gave me changed my outlook on life completely. You then said to me all she keeps saying is "After life is real, after life is real"!

You then joked she's describing what it's like, I've never had anyone show me this before. You then went on to say I would do a speech at the funeral and how I would get my mums engagement ring etc. I did! You then told me I would meet someone in uniform and his name would begin with "D".

I met Dave in the Army but then after that he left me. I saw you last night and you asked me, "Have you ditched the Army guy Dave?"

"GOOD! He was no good for you"! But you will be with someone in Uniform." I'll keep waiting on that one!

Another thing had happened when my mum was ill and no one knew she was sitting on the stairs and goes to me "Ella where am I?

I said, "you're at home you Wally". She was sick and she was having problems with her head.

You told me this story and my mum and I were the only ones there!

You said to me, "all your mum keeps saying is remember the incident on the stairs"! It wasn't funny then, but it is now.

You also done a tarot card reading on me and produced a card with a devil on which I automatically didn't like seeing that one! As most would! You told me someone will enter my life who isn't very nice. I met a guy who manipulated me with a distinctive number plate with 666 within it!

I cannot begin to describe how much you have helped me with my grief and I will continue to book readings with you for the rest of my life because you are truly gifted!

And you have helped me spiritually."

"I arrived for the sitting more in curiosity than any deep need to contact my non-living family and I was more than sceptical.

I remember thinking "What am I doing here? I am a man of logic and science a devout atheist, I have A levels in Maths and Physics, WHAT am I doing here?"

Stephanie is lovely. That word is overused these days and rarely *really* applies to a human being but she just is. There is warmth and a genuine sense of 'good person' about her. This annoyed me because I wanted to dislike her. I wanted her to be wrong about everything so I could walk away with my faith in science and the status quo smugly intact.

I will not reveal the content of the sitting because it is very personal but I will reveal how a cold sweat enveloped me as certain details emanated from this softly spoken, lovely lady.

Am I converted? Is there life after death?

Well, when Stephanie said 'There'll be news of a baby in the family within a year', my wife and I smiled to each other. This was biologically impossible. Got her!

I write this as a brand new grandfather. Charlie was born ten days ago. The news of his arrival came nine months after my sitting. James (Ipswich)"

"When talking to friends about the afterlife, the question is always raised, well do you believe? I have always said that I do due to the experience of my relatives. I have never had proof of my own, that was until you came round on the 20th November 2009. For you to have said the things you did to my Aunt, I was stunned, amazed and just so thrilled that there is 100% proof. I needed to say yes I do believe in the afterlife, listen to my experience with Stephanie.

I am still singing your praises on a weekly basis, by the time I'm finished I think everyone will know who Stephanie Carr is!"

"Hi Steph

I'm one of the ladies you saw last night at Sally's house. I got your email from Sally because I wanted to thank you for possibly saving my life!

You mentioned that I should get my car tyre pressure checked as you had seen a picture of the car and wheels being pointed out to you. I took the car into a tyre place this morning and while I was there, asked the mechanic if he'd check my hand brake light which has been permanently on but the hand brake has been off. He looked at me as if I was a bit "doolally" and said, "If it's permanently on, it means you might have a brake problem!" He said he could fit the car in Thursday but meanwhile would just do a quick check.

He discovered I had no brake fluid and the car wasn't safe to drive! It's turned out that the rear brake fluid pipe near the wheels has fractured and was pumping out brake fluid. I needed the whole thing replaced urgently which he's doing as I write. I had been previously told that the light being on was most likely just a minor electrical fault with the bulb on the dashboard and wouldn't have gone into the garage for ages if it hadn't been for your message yesterday.

Feeling a bit spooked by it, but VERY VERY grateful.
 Many thanks,
 Karen"

"On the morning of the 31st of August 2016 my wife was booked for a reading with Stephanie but due to illness she was unable to make it , So I attended in her place instead I was greeted at the front door by Stephanie, she ushered me into the dining room where I sat down , I was then asked to shuffle the card's which Stephanie gave me, she then placed the card's in the sign of the cross in front of me, after that Stephanie explained my card reading.

To my amazement she told me in the reading something only our family members would know which made me think she was the teller of truth I then sat in a cool state of mind, Firstly in the reading my dear father came through and after a short time my father let another young male into the reading and from what Stephanie was telling me this person sounded very familiar then I was asked by Stephanie who was Richard? To which I answered he's my oldest son, she then asked me was the young male related to me and I said yes I think he is, I was then asked about a motorcycle picture to which I answered yes that makes sense.

I was then asked did I have a tattoo in memory of the young male. I said yes I do. Stephanie then said is this young male your son to which brought a lump to my throat and filled my eyes with tears.

My son had been involved in a motorcycle accident and had passed over. Stephanie then asked who George was. I then told her where George fitted into the reading and things were all falling into place, I was given dates and names which was all relevant, Stephanie then asked me about an item that belonged to our son in the garage I said yes there is something that belonged to him still in there which hasn't been moved since his passing, then she told me that our son said never to sell or get rid of it, this won't happen I told her.

By this time I had been at the reading for around fifty five minutes I was so pleased by what Stephanie had told me it was just like having treatment for pain but there was No pain it felt as though a burden was lifted from me I felt at ease from hearing the message from the loving son of ours Stephanie then said he was happy and would be close to the family. Stephanie then asked me if my wife spent any time in our late Son's bedroom to which I said yes she does, Stephanie said well that is where he is close to her.

We have had some strange things that have occurred since his passing and they all fit in with our son Rhys.

I would like to say that in my opinion the messages sent via Stephanie were all so close to the heart she is a very talented women with a very special gift it was so comforting to be in the presence of Stephanie.

Richard (Ipswich)"

The Poem I Wrote for Mum

If I could share a day with you,
I would do everything I dreamed we would
do,
to tell you how important you are to me,
and hold you so close, so you could see,
all of these things I should have done,
when you was on earth as my mum,
but we all make our plans on borrowed time,
and the future for us is no longer mine,
you had your own destiny and pathway to go,
and I miss you darling like you would never
know,
the ties that bonded us both from the past,
are the ties of love that forever will last,
my only regret now you are not here,
is I should have told you how I love you so
dear,
so I hope you hear my prayers today,
as I write with love that we meet someday,
so I can take you by the hand,
as we walk together in Gods holy land,
then all my grieving would have been
worthwhile,
to see your face, and watch you smile.

This was my mum at my age (53)

A Note To My Readers

I am and always will be forever grateful for all my mum did to love and protect me.

People ask me now if I believe in religion or God? And I answer that I used to believe in religion, but life has shown me that really that comes down to what part of the world you was born in to what religion you will follow, and that one should not be right or over shadow the other. Life has also shown me that it is the biggest subject to create and bring war between mankind, when indeed any religion should practise peace to the world.

I do however believe in a God, a higher power of energy that is pure love. I believe we don't need to hide behind a religion to be a good person. In fact some of the nicest kindest people I know are atheist.

So my religion is to take personal responsibility for who you are, and to be the very best and kindest person you can be.

If you can look at yourself in the mirror, and like the person and all you stand for looking back at you, then in my mind you're not doing too bad.

People will remember you by the love, kindness, and difference you brought to them, to me that in itself is priceless

Some people ask me, "Are you a Medium, Fortune Teller, or Psychic, Stephanie?"

My answer is, "I am none of these,

I am just an Ordinary Girl, with an extra Ordinary Gift."

Dear Reader

If you have enjoyed reading my book then please tell your friends and relatives and leave a review on Amazon and Goodreads.
Thank you.

About the Author

Stephanie Carr is a well-known and respected psychic and clairvoyant medium, who has spent nearly thirty years demonstrating her gift to sell-out audiences around the country, as well as appearing frequently on BBC radio.

She is very much a people person, keen on socialising and getting to know people both through her work and leisure activities.

When she is not working, she loves nothing better than cooking for, and being surrounded by, her family. She also enjoys walking her two bearded collies, and attending agility training classes with them. She can often be found pottering in her garden.

She is currently working on a second book covering her later life and work.

To find out more about Stephanie, please visit:
Website: www.stephaniecarr.co.uk

Facebook Author Page:
https://www.facebook.com/Stephanie-Carr-Author-763001923841295/?fref=ts

To my Dear friend Kim,

Hope you Enjoyed my
Book.
Love Always
        Steph x